Preschool

By: Ken Carder & Sue LaRoy

Illustrations: Adam Severin & Dan Zola

Cover Illustration: Tammy Ortner

Easily use these learning songs, worksheets, and activities with kids of all learning styles!

Many kids are **visual learners.** They think in pictures, quickly converting everything they read, see, and hear into images in their mind. Most visual learners can sit still at their desk easily, focus for longer periods of time, and turn in neat, organized work. Visual learners are more comfortable learning from workbooks and textbooks.

Other children are **auditory learners.** These kids don't do what visual learners seem to do naturally. Auditory learners learn best by listening —being read to, listening to audio books, discussing a topic one-on-one with a teacher or within a small group, singing and learning with music and rhythm.

Still other children are **kinesthetic learners** who learn best through a hands-on approach, body movement, activities, arts and crafts, and manipulating objects.

These songs, worksheets and activities are easily adaptable for use both at home or in the classroom. Parents and caregivers may jumpstart or reinforce school learning at home with the fun, family activities. Classroom teachers may adapt the activities and worksheets as a supplement to their curriculum.

www.twinsisters.com

1-800-248-TWIN (8946)

Twin Sisters Productions, LLC • Akron, OH

Credits:
Publisher: Twin Sisters Productions, LLC
Executive Producers: Kim Mitzo Thompson,
Karen Mitzo Hilderbrand
Music by: Kim Mitzo Thompson, Karen Mitzo Hilderbrand, and Hal Wright except the following: *If You're Happy And You Know It, The Wheels On The Bus, Down By The Bay,* and *Ten In The Bed.*
Music Arranged by: Hal Wright
Workbook Authors: Ken Carder, Sue LaRoy
Book Design: Angelee Randlett, Christine Della Penna
Illustrations: Adam Severin, Dan Zola
Cover Illustration: Tammy Ortner

ISBN 1575838176

Twin Sisters Productions, LLC
1-800-248-8946 www.twinsisters.com

About the Authors

Ken Carder (Author, Editor)

Ken is a graduate of The University of Akron in Akron, OH with a BA in Communication And Rhetoric, and of Evangelical School of Theology in Myerstown, PA with a M-Div. For the past three years Ken has worked exclusively with Twin Sisters Productions to develop new educational music resources for children. He and his wife have worked extensively with young children in churches, summer camps, schools, a syndicated radio ministry broadcast, and community theater. Ken and his wife are proud parents of three children, Stephen, Nathan, and McKenna.

Sue LaRoy (Author)

Sue has been in the field of education for over 30 years. Her varied involvement has included the classroom, sales, marketing and product development. She started out in Early Childhood Education as a teacher and curriculum coordinator and was instrumental in creating an alternative arts program for elementary teachers. She went on to develop an award-winning, nationally recognized program which effectively partnered businesses and their resources with schools in their communities. For the past 12 years, Sue has been a consultant developing educational products for a number of manufacturers and publishers.

TABLE OF CONTENTS

Make learning *FUN* for your four–and five–year old with the music, family activities, mini-books, worksheets, flashcards, and games in Preschool Songs That Teach Workbook Set.

Sing, move, play, and learn with the songs on the accompanying music CD. Preschool children love to sing, wiggle, march, jump, and clap to music. Incorporate these learning songs throughout your child's daily routine. You'll be amazed at how quickly your child will be singing along and learning, too.

Introduce or reinforce skills your child is learning in preschool with the **family activities, emergent reader mini-books, worksheets, flashcards,** and **games.** You'll have fun learning:

- *Alphabet and Pre-reading*
- *Numbers and Counting*
- *Colors and Shapes*
- *Days of the Week*
- *Responsibility and Kindness*
- *Dressing*
- *Animals and Sounds*

Above all, enjoy your time with your child knowing that the time you spend together now is laying a foundation for learning and future success in kindergarten and beyond!

Sincerely,

Kim Thompson

Kim Mitzo Thompson

Karen Hilderbrand

Karen Mitzo Hilderbrand

Twin Sisters Productions, LLC

Alphabet & Letters

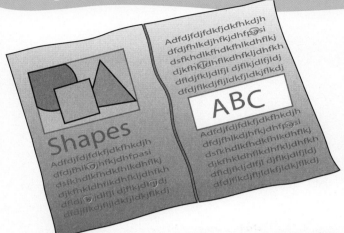

Letters in the News

Read the daily newspaper with your child. Choose a letter of the alphabet and ask your child to find and circle as many of that letter as he can find on a page of the newspaper. Say the letter and read the words your child finds.

Letter of the Week ...or of the Day!

Throughout your daily routine focus on one selected letter of the alphabet. Suppose you choose this week as "C" week or "C" day!

- During meal time or snack time identify any foods that start with C
- While playing in the park, name anything you see that starts with C
- Think of any family, friends, or pets whose name begins with C
- Practice writing or drawing pictures of items that start with C

Pretzel Letters

Follow this simple recipe to make pretzel dough. Together, shape a small ball of dough to form a letter of the alphabet. Make the "Letter of the Week" or all the letters of the alphabet.

1 package yeast	1 beaten egg
4 cups flour	1 tsp Salt
1 1/2 cup warm water	1 Tbsp Sugar

Measure water in a mixing bowl. Sprinkle yeast in the water. Add salt, sugar, and flour. Mix and knead dough approximately 3 minutes. Grease cookie sheets. Shape the pretzel dough into letters and lay them on the cookie sheets. Brush the dough letters with beaten egg, and sprinkle them with salt. Bake at 425 degrees for 12-15 minutes. After the pretzels have cooled, share the alphabet treats with your friends and family.

Sandwich Art

Spread peanut butter, cream cheese, or a favorite sandwich spread on a piece of bread. Then let your child write a letter of the alphabet on the bread using raisins, banana slices, crackers, celery, carrot slices, chocolate chips, strawberries, orange segments, pretzel sticks, etc.

Clay Alphabet & Numbers

Make letters or numbers out of homemade play dough or modeling clay.

Bob for Letters, Numbers, or Shapes

Cut numbers, shapes, and uppercase or lowercase letters out of construction paper or use the Alphabet Cards on pages 11–13. Place a loop of masking tape on each one. Place the cutouts in a large clothesbasket, box, or pan. Bob for letters, numbers or shapes by touching your nose to the masking tape! To win, your child must identify the letter, number or shape. For more challenging play, bob for a specific letter, number, or shape.

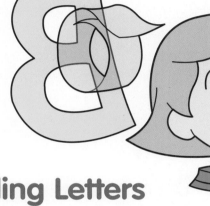

Cheerleading Letters

Simply call out in cheering fashion, asking for the letters of your child's name—or any other new word—one at a time. For example, parent, "Give me a K!" Child, "K!" "Give me an I!" "I." "Give me a M!" "M!" "What does that spell?" Together, "Kim!"

C is for Cow

Keep an ongoing scrapbook of pictures starting with each letter of the alphabet. Cut pictures from magazines, junk mail, and catalogs. Use a three-ring binder, spiral notebook, or even a hardcover blank journal.

Alphabet Guessing

Place inexpensive magnetic letters and numbers in a paper bag or shoebox. Players close their eyes and pick a magnetic letter out of a paper bag. To win the letter, the player must identify the letter. For more challenging play, try to identify the letter by feeling it, with your eyes closed.

Swamp

Toss socks or fabric scraps around the room—these are the alligators. At one end of the room place the Alphabet Cards (pages 11-13), number or shape cut outs. See how quickly your child can hop through the swamp, pick up a specific alphabet card, number, or shape, and make her way back—all without disturbing one of the pretend alligators.

Tightrope Walker

Make one or several large letters on the floor with masking tape. Challenge your preschooler to walk the "tightrope" and identify the letter. You try it first, by walking on the tape without stepping off. Then let your preschooler have a turn, and see if he can stay on the tape better than you can.

Mystery Writing

While your child holds out his hand and closes his eyes, write a letter on his hand with your finger. He tries to guess what you're writing. Start with just letters, then with two- or three-letter words.

The Alphabet Game

During short drives around town or longer road trips, search together for words beginning with a selected letter. Look on street signs, buildings, passing trucks, etc. For more challenging play, search for words beginning with each letter of the alphabet in order. (You may want to agree to search for words that contain the letters Q, X, and Z.)

Alphabet March

Write one letter of the alphabet on a piece of construction or copy paper. Play with all 26 letters or any that your child needs to drill. Place alphabet cards on the floor forming a circle. Play your favorite song while your child steps on each alphabet card. When you stop the music, he must freeze in place and say the name of the letter he is standing on. Remove that letter, as in musical chairs, and repeat until one letter remains.

Letter Search

Use the Alphabet Cards on pages 11-13. Send your child in search of alphabet cards you've hidden around the house. Each time he finds a letter he must return to you and say the letter aloud. Reward him with a small prize for finding all the letters.

Alphabet Mix 'n' Match

Cut apart the alphabet cards on pages 11-13. The object of the memory game is to match the uppercase and lowercase versions of each letter. Place each card face down. Take turns lifting two cards, trying to find the uppercase and lowercase pair.

Alphabet Tic Tac Toe

Instead of an X and an O, play with lowercase b and d, which are among the more difficult letters for children to recognize because they look so similar. Or choose any two letters your child might be having trouble identifying, or let your child choose any two letters she likes.

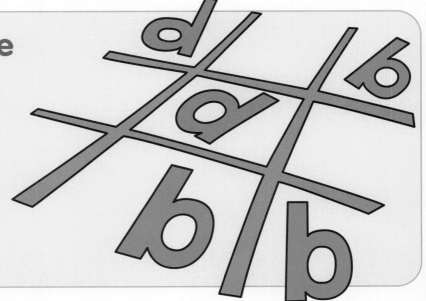

Alphabet Shopping

Create a pretend shopping list together. Choose two letters that have very different sounds, such as M and D. Divide a paper into two columns and write uppercase M on top of one column and uppercase D on top of the other. Search store advertisements for items that begin with the selected letter Cut out the picture and glue it onto the shopping list in the correct column.

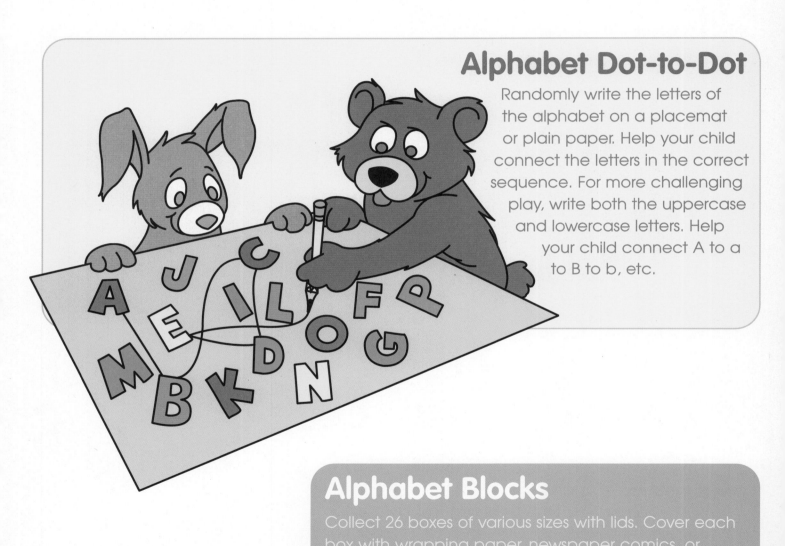

Alphabet Dot-to-Dot

Randomly write the letters of the alphabet on a placemat or plain paper. Help your child connect the letters in the correct sequence. For more challenging play, write both the uppercase and lowercase letters. Help your child connect A to a to B to b, etc.

Alphabet Blocks

Collect 26 boxes of various sizes with lids. Cover each box with wrapping paper, newspaper comics, or construction paper. Write an uppercase and/or lowercase letter on each box. Help your child build and sequence the alphabet blocks. Perhaps you can store treasures in each box that begin with that letter.

Alphabet Cards for use with activities on pages 8-10.

A B C D
E F G H
I J K L
M N O P
Q R S T
U V W X
Y Z

This page was intentionally left blank for "Alphabet Cards" activities to be completed.

a b c d

e f g h

i j k l

m n o p

q r s t

u v w x

y z

This page was intentionally left blank for "Alphabet Cards" activities to be completed.

Alphabet Gallery

Line the walls of your play area, bedroom, or classroom with homemade Alphabet Posters. Draw an outline of each uppercase letter on individual sheets of poster board, construction paper, or copy paper. Over a period of time, decorate each Alphabet Poster by drawing pictures, writing words, gluing natural things or pictures cut from magazines and catalogs that begin with that letter. Look over these suggestions.

A – apples, ant, airplane, alligator, angels, anchor

B – buttons, Band-aid, beans, banana, bubble-wrap, black, blue, butterflies, bugs

C – circles, clown, car, caterpillar, cow, cup, camel, crocodile, cookies, coconut, carrot, circle

D – diamonds, pictures of daddy, doughnut, dog, dish, doll, dinosaur, duck

E – eggshells, envelope, elephant

F – family pictures, flowers, fan, feet, fish, firefighter, football, farm, fireworks, fruit

G – green, gloves, goat, glasses, gift, guitar, groundhog, grapes, gorilla

H – handprint, hat, pictures of your house, hammer, hen, horse, hippopotamus, ham, hook, heart

I – ice cream, igloo, iguana, insects, island, icicle, ice cube, ice skates

J – jams, jelly labels, jean fabric swatches, jacks, jellybeans, jell-o®, jumprope

K – kittens, kites, Kool-aid®, kazoos, key, kiwi, kangaroo, king

L – leaves, lace, lines, lightning, lemon, lion, lamb, lips

M – marbles, music, monkey, milk, music, mitten, mask, mop, man, mailbox, melon, meat, mushroom

N – nuts, noodles, newspaper, nurse, nickel, net, nail, needle, number

O – orange, octopus, oval, overalls, ocean, ostrich, otter, ox

P – pasta, pigs, pinecones, pockets, photographs, pink, purple, police officer,

Q – queen, quilts

R – rose petals, rocks, red, rocket, ruler, reindeer, rainbow, rectangle, rollercoaster, rake, ring

S – string, soap, sponges, snowflakes, square, star, spider, snail, snake, sand

T – teal or turquoise, tent, table, tree, tea, teapot, turkey, teddy bear, tomato, triangle

U – umbrellas, up, under, uncle

V – violins, violet, valentine, volcano, van, vacuum, vegetable

W – wild animals, white, wagon, watermelon, wood, windmill, window, web, woodpecker, water,

X – x-ray, xylophone, fox, box, T-rex, six *(you may find it easier to search for words that **end** in x.)*

Y – yellow, yarn, yardsticks, yo-yo, yogurt, yell, yolk

Z – zoo animals, zippers, zero, zucchini

Alphabet or Number Derby

Tear out and tape together the game board pages. To play, you will need one die, and a game piece for each player—small candies, cereal, coins, or tokens from other games. Players take turns rolling the die and moving a game piece as many spaces as the number thrown. To remain on that space, the player must quickly identify the number, uppercase letter, or lowercase letter on that space. The first player to reach "FINISH" is the winner.

How To Make the Mini-Books

The seven mini-books coordinate with the fun learning songs on the companion CD. Work together to color, assemble, "read," and sing the mini-books.

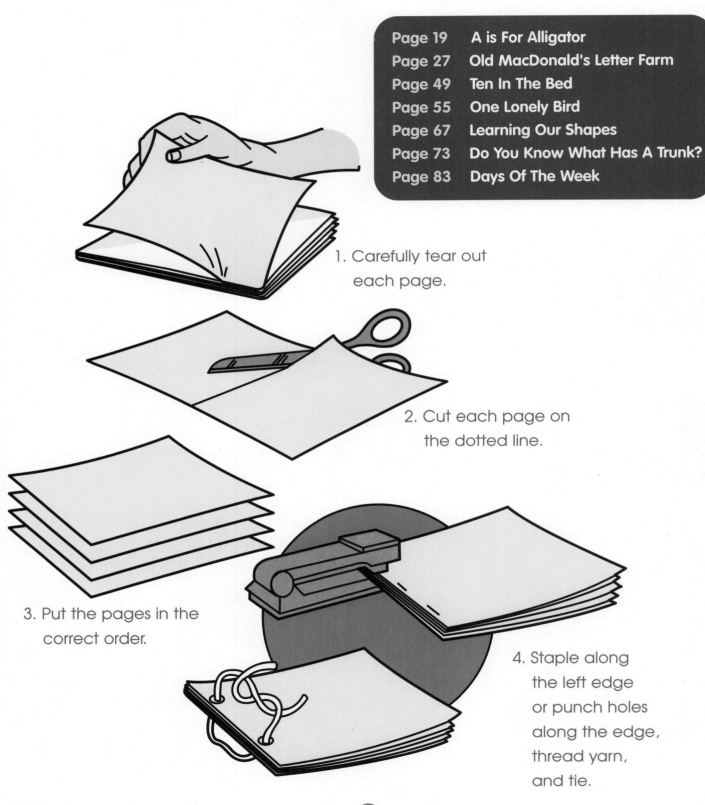

1. Carefully tear out each page.

2. Cut each page on the dotted line.

3. Put the pages in the correct order.

4. Staple along the left edge or punch holes along the edge, thread yarn, and tie.

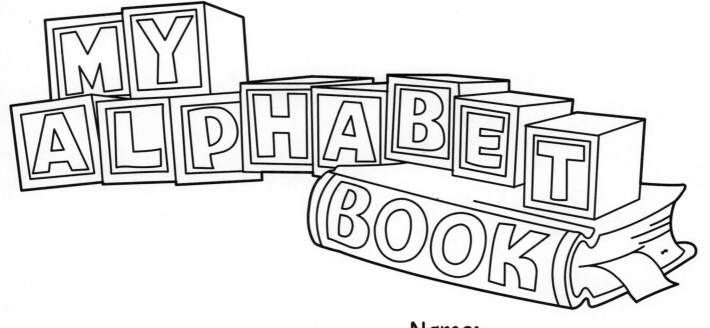

Name:

_____

_ _ _ _ _ _ _ _ _ _ _ _ _ _ _ _ _ _ _ _

_____

Song:
A Is For Alligator (Track 2)

1

C c

C is for caterpillar.

D d

D is for doll.

D is for doll.

3

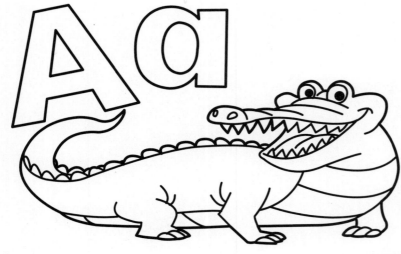

Aa

A is for alligator.

B is for ball.

Bb

2

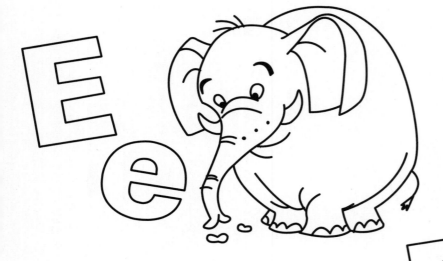

E e

E is for elephant.

F is for frog.

Ff

4

G is for goat.

H is for hog.

5

K is for kitten.

L is for lamb.

7

Ii

I is for **igloo.**

Jj

J is for **jam.**

6

Mm

M is for **mittens.**

Nn

N is for **nail.**

8

O O

O is for
octopus.

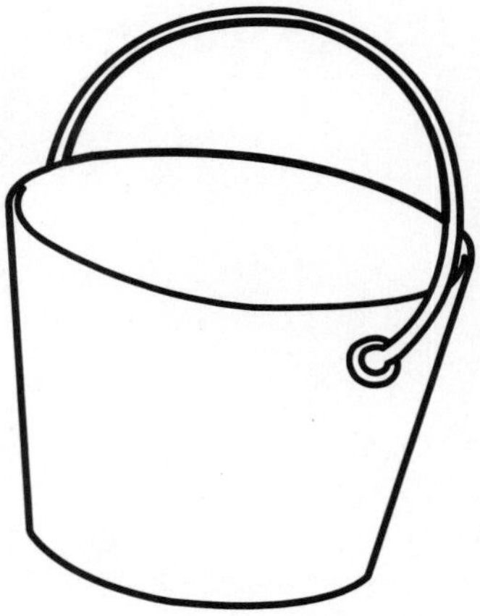

P is for **pail.**

P p

9

S

S

S is for
sailboat.

T is for **toad.**

T t

11

Q q

UNITED STATES OF AMERICA
QUARTER DOLLAR

Q is for
quarter.

R r

R is for **road.**

10

U u

U is for
umbrella.

V v

V is for **vine.**

12

W is for **worms** who wiggle all the time.

13

Y is for **yes.**

15

X is for **x-ray.**

14

Z is for **ZOO.** We're through, I guess!

16

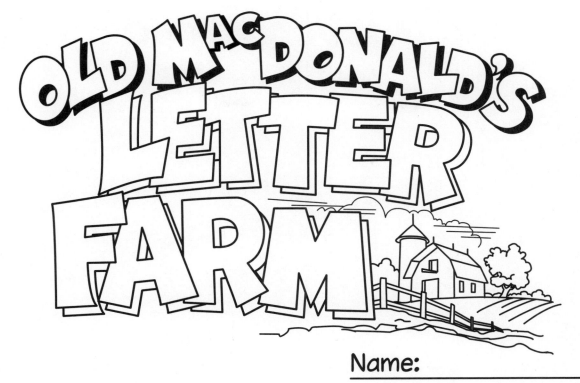

OLD MacDONALD'S LETTER FARM

Name: _____

_____

_____

Song:
Old MacDonald's Letter Farm
(Track 3)

1

3

Old MacDonald had a farm.

2

Letters, letters in the hay.

4

5

7

With a

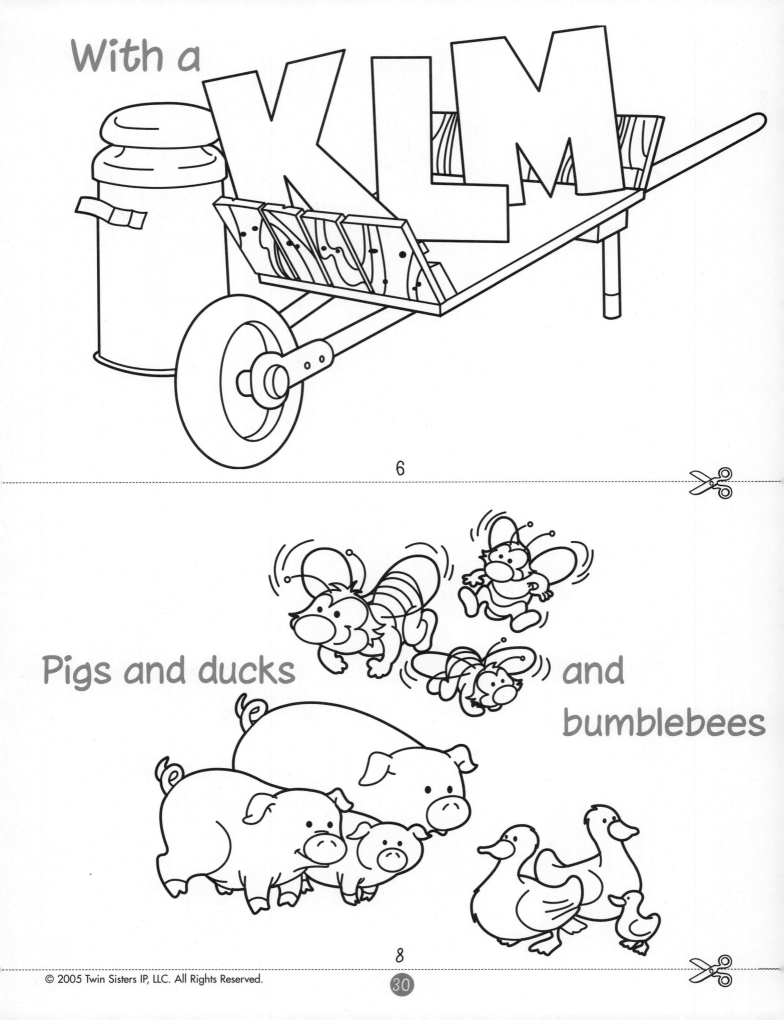

6

Pigs and ducks and bumblebees

8

9

11

10

Old MacDonald had a farm.

12

Uppercase-Lowercase Matching

Draw a line from the uppercase letter to its matching lowercase letter.

E

G

B

M

L

T

W

Uppercase-Lowercase Matching

Draw a line from the uppercase letter to its matching lowercase letter.

P
Y
F
N
A
R
S

n
a
p
s
f
y
r

Uppercase Rainbow Letters

Trace each **uppercase alphabet letter** with a colored pencil. Trace each letter again with a different colored pencil. Repeat several times to create Rainbow Letters.

Alphabet & Letters

Lowercase Rainbow Letters

Trace each **lowercase alphabet letter** with a colored pencil. Trace each letter again with a different colored pencil. Repeat several times to create Rainbow Letters.

Write Your Own Uppercase Rainbow Letters

Write each **uppercase alphabet letter** with a colored pencil. Write each letter again with a different colored pencil. Repeat several times to create Rainbow Letters.

Write Your Own Lowercase Rainbow Letters

Write each **lowercase alphabet letter** with a colored pencil. Write each letter again with a different colored pencil. Repeat several times to create Rainbow Letters.

Missing Letters

Write the letter that comes next.

A, B, _____

L, M, _____

T, U, _____

Write the letter that comes first.

_____ E, F

_____ Q, R

_____ Y, Z

Write the missing letters.

A _ C D E _ G _ I

J _ L M _ _ O P _

R S _ U V _ X _ Z

Dot-to-Dot, A-Z

Color By Letter

a= Blue   i= Green   u= Yellow
e= Pink   o= Brown

Numbers & Counting

Songs
• One Lonely Bird- #19
• How Many Ducks- #20
• Counting To Ten- #21
• Ten In The Bed- #22

Easy, Fun Activities to Teach Children Numbers and Counting

Number of the Week ...or of the day!

Throughout your daily routine focus on one selected number. Suppose you choose this week as "8" week or "8" day:

• Begin the day with Number 8 Pancakes (see page 43)
• Search the newspaper for number 8
• Gather and sort numerous collections of 8 items each
• Decide on a silly sound or gesture you'll make each time you see a number 8

Number Workout

Take turns rolling a die. On your turn, identify the number on top of the die and then choose an exercise that both of you will do that number of times! Be certain to count aloud. For more challenging play use two dice.

Newspaper Numbers

Help your child search for numbers on a page of the daily newspaper. Identify each number and circle it with a marker or highlighter.

Beanbag Toss

Draw a tic-tac-toe grid on a large piece of paper or on the sidewalk with chalk. Write one number in each area. Help your preschooler toss a beanbag and identify the number on which it lands. Play tic-tac-toe with several beanbags of different colors.

I Spy a Number!

Walk together through the house, grocery store, or the neighborhood searching for objects that feature numbers—appliances, clocks, calendars, boxes and containers, house numbers, street signs.

Sand Writing

Fill a cookie sheet or shallow box with sand—salt will work, too. Say a number and have your preschooler try to write that number in the sand using a finger.

Number Rubbings

Cut numbers out of sandpaper. Cover the sandpaper numbers with copy paper and rub them with crayons. Begin with only one cutout and help your preschooler identify the number. Later, add more number cutouts and make a colorful design.

Number Pancakes

Prepare and pour pancake batter into a squeeze bottle. Squirt the batter onto a hot griddle to form the number your child selects. Of course, when the number pancakes are ready you'll have a tasty breakfast treat. But before you eat the pancakes you'll have to identify the number and clap your hands that many times.

Jellybean Math

Pass out twenty jellybeans. Count the jellybeans aloud together. Have your preschooler sort each jellybean by color. Now, count the red jellybeans. Next, count pink jellybeans, green jellybeans, and so on. For more challenging play, make different patterns using the jellybeans. Or introduce the concept of "How many more" by helping your child count four red jellybeans, three pink jellybeans, and seeing the difference. Make up story problems your preschooler can begin to answer by manipulating the jellybeans.

Rainbow Numbers

Trace each number with a colored pencil. Trace each number again with a different colored pencil. Repeat several times to create Rainbow Numbers.

Write Your Own Rainbow Numbers

Write the **numbers 1-10** with a colored pencil. Write each number again with a different colored pencil. Repeat several times to create Rainbow Numbers.

Learning Numbers 1-10

Write the numbers 1 - 10.

_____

- -

_____

- -

_____

Write the number that comes next.

1, 2, _____

3, 4, _____

5, 6, _____

7, 8, _____

Write the number that comes first.

_____ 3, 4

_____ 7, 8

_____ 9, 10

_____ 2, 3

Write the missing numbers.

1, 2, ___, 4, 5, ___, 7, ___, ___, 10

Dot-to-Dot, 1-20

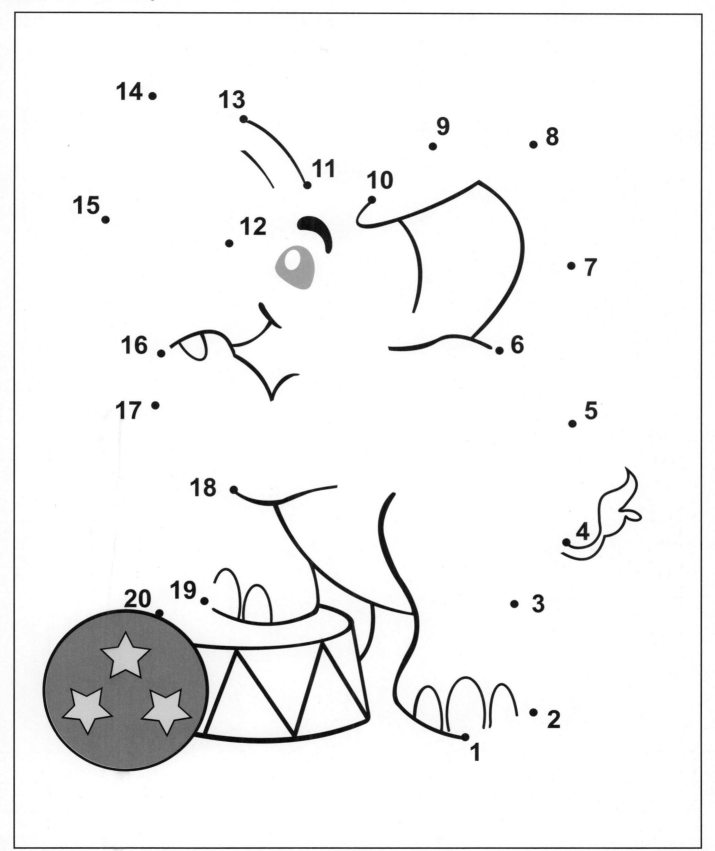

Color By Number

1= Black	**2= Green**	**3= Brown**	**4= Yellow**
5= Red	**6= Orange**	**7= Blue**	**8= Purple**

TEN IN THE BED

Name: _____

_ _ _ _ _ _ _ _ _ _ _ _ _

_____

Song:
Ten In The Bed (Track 22)

1

There were NINE in the bed and the little one said, "Roll over, roll over." So they all rolled over and one fell out.

Trace and write.

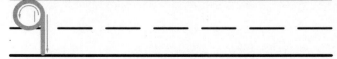

3

49

There were TEN in the bed and the little one said, "Roll over, roll over." So they all rolled over and one fell out.

2

Trace and write.

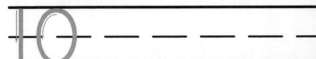

There were EIGHT in the bed and the little one said, "Roll over, roll over." So they all rolled over and one fell out.

4

Trace and write.

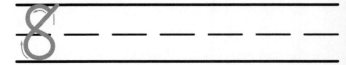

There were SEVEN in the bed and the little one said, "Roll over, roll over." So they all rolled over and one fell out.

5

Trace and write.

7

There were FIVE in the bed and the little one said, "Roll over, roll over." So they all rolled over and one fell out.

7

Trace and write.

5

There were SIX in the bed and the little one said, "Roll over, roll over." So they all rolled over and one fell out.

6

Trace and write.

6 _ _ _ _ _ _ _ _ _

There were FOUR in the bed and the little one said, "Roll over, roll over." So they all rolled over and one fell out.

8

Trace and write.

4 _ _ _ _ _ _ _ _ _

There were THREE in the bed and the little one said, "Roll over, roll over." So they all rolled over and one fell out.

9

Trace and write.

3 _ _ _ _ _ _ _ _

There was ONE in the bed and the little one said, "Good night!"

11

Trace and write.

There were TWO in the bed and the little one said, "Roll over, roll over." So they all rolled over and one fell out.

10

Trace and write.

2 — — — — — — —

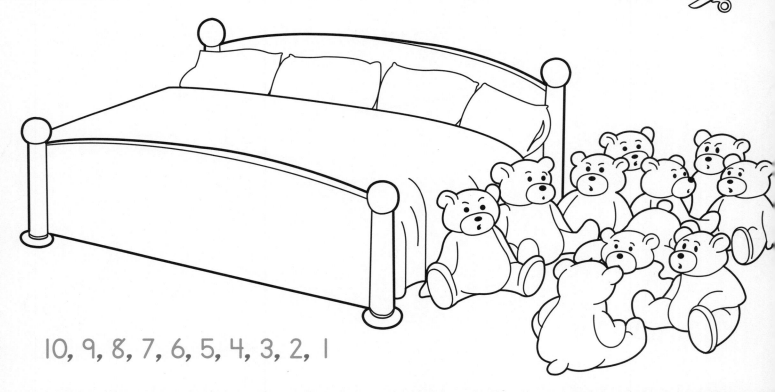

10, 9, 8, 7, 6, 5, 4, 3, 2, 1

10 9 8 7 6 5 4 3 2 1

12

ONE LONELY BIRD

Name:

Song:
One Lonely Bird (Track 19)

1

Another bird came by to sing. Now two little birds were sitting in the tree.

3

One lonely bird was sitting in a tree.
"I need a friend to sing with me."

2

Trace and write.

Two little birds were sitting in a tree.
"We need a friend to sing on key."

4

Trace and write.

2

Another bird came by to sing. Now THREE little birds were sitting in the tree.

5

Another bird came by to sing. Now FOUR little birds were sitting in the tree.

7

Three little birds were sitting in a tree.
"We need a friend to sing on key."

Trace and write.

3 - - - - - - - - - -

6

Four little birds were sitting in a tree.
"We need a friend to sing on key."

Trace and write.

4 - - - - - - - - - -

8

Another bird came by to sing. Now
FIVE little birds were sitting in a tree.   9

The birds flew away unable to sing.   11

Five little birds were sitting in a tree.
All five birds sang off key.

Trace and write.

5

10

One lonely bird still stayed in the tree.

12

Songs
- **Colors- #7**
- **Froggy, You're So Green- #8**

Easy, Fun Activities to Teach Children Colors and Shapes

Color of the Day ...or of the Week

Pick a color for the day. Wear everything of that color, eat that color, and play with that color. Focus on the selected color throughout your daily routine. Suppose you choose this day as "Green Day" or this week as "Green Week:"

- Wear green clothes
- During meal time or snack time make and eat any green foods
- While playing in the park, name anything you see that is green
- Play only with green toys
- Count green road and building signs
- Draw pictures of things that are green

Color-coded Road Trip

Choose a color before heading out on a short road trip. As the cars pass, watch for the cars of that particular color and give a shout or cheer! Older children can count how many cars of each color go by.

Color Shopping

Pick a color. Go from room to room in the house looking for objects to put in your basket or box that are the color you picked. Unload the basket naming each item and repeating each color.

Watercolor Rainbow

Paint a rainbow in the correct order of color—red, orange, yellow, green, blue, and purple—with very thin watercolor paint. Sprinkle salt on the rainbow while the paint is still wet, and the colors will run together.

Ice Cream Treat

Visit an old-fashioned ice cream shop—one with many different kinds of ice cream visible in the freezer. Help your child identify the colors of each flavor. Then treat yourselves to a cone or sundae!

Color Mixing Fun

Three primary colors—red, yellow, and blue—make up all the other colors in the world. Mixing the primary colors in various combinations will create all other colors—called secondary colors.

For example:
Yellow + Red = Orange
Red + Blue = Violet
Blue + Yellow = Green

Cookies or Cupcakes

Have fun together while experiencing the "magic" of color mixing with this yummy treat.

You'll need:
- Vanilla cake frosting (store bought or homemade)
- Red, yellow, and blue food coloring
- Bowls or paper plates
- Cookies or cupcakes

In separate containers, mix each primary color frosting by adding the food coloring to the vanilla icing. Work together to frost cookies or cupcakes with the three primary colors. Next, on a paper plate or in a small bowl, help your child to mix small amounts of the yellow and blue icing. Can your child predict what color frosting will result? Spread the icing on more cookies or cupcakes. Repeat, mixing blue and red icing, then red and yellow icing.

Color Mixing Discovery Bottles

Shake and make both primary and secondary colors!

You'll need:
- Three empty, clear plastic bottles
- Water
- Vegetable oil
- Red, yellow, and blue food coloring
- Red, yellow, and blue tempera paint powder
- Tape or Glue

First, partially fill three clear plastic bottles with water. Add food coloring to each bottle—one red, one yellow, and another blue. Next, pour vegetable oil into three separate cups or containers. Mix one color of dry tempera paint powder in each container of vegetable oil—one red, one yellow, and another blue. Pour one of the tempera paint color mixtures into each plastic bottle partially filled with water of a different color. To prevent spills, glue or tape the cap onto the bottle. When lightly shaken the colors will mix to form a secondary color, and then separate into the two primary colors.

Shape and Color Patterning

Work together to cut out shapes in a variety of sizes and colors from construction paper or craft foam. You'll need quite a few cut out shapes! To play, make a simple pattern by laying the shapes on the table or floor. Say, "I see a pattern, do you?" Help your child to identify the pattern. Then help your child recreate the pattern using additional shape cutouts, identifying each shape and color when placing it into the pattern. Store the shapes in a plastic storage bag for play while waiting at restaurants, doctors offices, and brief moments of down time.

What Color Am I?

For easy, quick reinforcement of color learning, play this simple game of clues! Say, "I am thinking of a color that is the color of the clouds. What color am I?" (White) "I am thinking of a color that is the color of the sun. What color am I?" (Yellow) "I am thinking of a color that is the color of grass. What color am I?" (Green) "I am thinking of a color that is the color of the sky. What color am I?" (Blue) "I am thinking of a color that is the color of a banana. What color am I?" (Yellow) "I am thinking of a color that is the color of an orange. What color am I?" (Orange)

63

Colorful Nonsense Sentences

Take turns completing a funny sentence until you both break out with silly giggles. For example, "I like big green..."—and then fill in the blank. "I like big green trees." "I like big green frogs." And then it starts to get silly—"I like big green cats!"

Color Dominos

Cut white poster board into 1– by 2– inch pieces. On each piece draw and color two shapes with markers. Use many different shapes and colors. Make the pieces look like dominos. Play as you would with regular dominos, matching color and shape together. You can also make dominos with uppercase and lowercase letters to reinforce alphabet learning. Store the homemade dominos in a plastic storage bag for play while waiting at restaurants, doctors' offices, and brief moments of down time.

Silly Sound Game

Make up silly sounds for different things you see during a short drive or long road trip. For example, say "Beep-beep" when you see a yellow car, "Ding-dong" when you see a church building, "Ho-ho-ho" when you see a red brick house, and "Honk-honk" when you see an orange truck.

Follow My Directions!

Cut large shapes out of various colors of construction paper and spread them close together on the floor. Ask your child to follow your directions and perform different actions. For example: put your foot on a red square. Jump over a purple circle. Put your hand on an orange triangle. For more fun, play with other family members or your child's friends. Add the rule that players must keep their hands or feet on the shape and color you specify until they all collapse.

Musical Shapes

Cut out shapes in various sizes and colors from poster board or construction paper. Or draw different shapes in a variety of colors on paper plates. To play, scatter the shapes on the floor in a large area. Play the companion Preschool Music CD while your child walks around the shapes. Stop the music and say "blue circle" or "red triangle" —or another shape and color you have chosen. Your child must find and stand on the appropriate shape. Continue the music, stop the music, and say another color and shape. Play this game with other family members or your child's friends, too. As in traditional musical chairs, players not standing on the appropriate shape must sit out the remainder of the game.

Shape Snack Fun!

Serve a fun snack made up of circles—Cheerios®, fruit ring cereal, apple rings, kiwi rings, banana slices. Serve square shaped snacks: wheat crackers, shortbread cookies, fruit chunks. Serve triangle shaped snacks: cheese slices, melon pieces. Or serve rectangles: cheese, carrot, or celery with dip. Before you eat, ask your child to identify the shapes. For more fun, put the shapes together to create a pattern or design.

Beanbag Toss

Make three or four beanbags by sewing scrap materials together and filling with beans, corn, or rice. Cut out shapes in various sizes and colors from poster board, construction paper, or craft foam. Ask your child to toss a beanbag onto a selected shape and/or color. You can also make beanbag toss targets using uppercase and lowercase letters to reinforce alphabet learning, or numbers 1 to 10 to reinforce number learning.

Colorful Ice Cubes

Together, fill an ice cube tray with water, add a few drops of food coloring to each square, and freeze to make several different colored cubes. Add them to a kiddy pool. Or drop a few cubes into the bathtub —try to catch them, describe the colors, watch them float, or watch them melt.

Edible Necklace

Give your child a piece of yarn with masking tape wrapped around each end. String colorful fruit-ring cereal. Help your child identify each color as she adds it to the necklace.

Shape And Color Treasure Hunt

Cut out shapes in various sizes and colors from poster board or construction paper. Hide the shapes around the house or classroom. Ask your child to search and find all the squares. Repeat with the other shapes and/or colors. Younger children can look for one item at a time and bring it to you. You may want to laminate each shape. You can also play "Hot and Cold" saying "hot, hotter, or hottest" or "cold, colder, coldest" as your child moves toward or away from a shape you've hidden in the room.

Driveway Hop

Color several large chalk shapes on the driveway or on the sidewalk. Have your child hop from the blue square to the green circle to the yellow triangle and then to the red heart, and so on.

Shape Tightrope

Make large outlines of a circle, square, triangle, and rectangle on the floor using masking tape. Help your child identify the shape before walking or hopping around its edges.

Dot-to-Dot Shapes

While waiting for your food to arrive at a restaurant, make dot-to-dot shapes on the placemat. Help your child connect the dots and identify the shape.

I Spy Shapes

Identify the shapes you see throughout your daily routine. Point out circle plates, rectangular trucks, square televisions, octagon stop signs, diamond-shaped kites, stars on signs, etc. For more challenging learning, play the classic game of "I Spy" with shapes.

Shape Collage

Cut shapes of many different kinds, sizes, and colors from construction paper. Help your child create a masterpiece by gluing the shapes onto a large piece of construction paper. Talk about the distinguishing features of each shape. Give varied instructions such as, glue the red square below the brown rectangle, or select one that is larger or smaller.

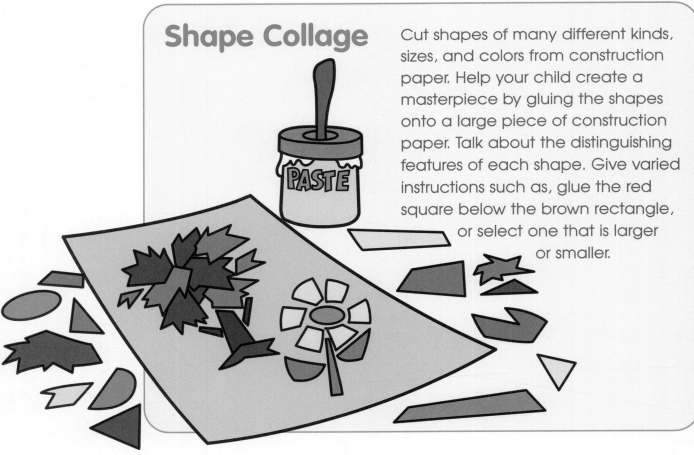

LEARNING OUR SHAPES

Song:
Learning Our Shapes (Track 9)

Name

1

A square has four sides.

3

Let's learn our shapes in school today.

2

All the sides
are equal.

_____

_____

_____

_____

4

A circle has no sides.

5

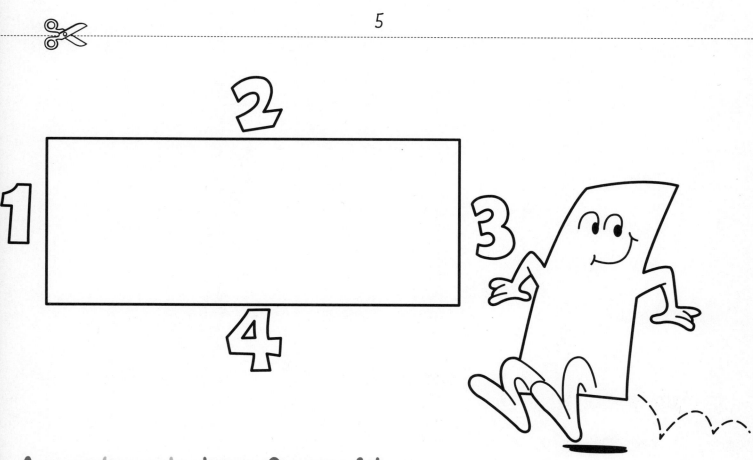

A rectangle has four sides.

7

It's shaped just like a ball.

6

Two sides are
long. Two sides
are short.

We've learned our
shapes today.

8

Animal Names & Sounds

Easy, Fun Activities to Teach Children
Animal Names and Sounds

Welcome to My Zoo

Help your child carefully place plush animals around the room, pretending it's a zoo. Let him take you on a tour of his zoo, making certain he identifies each animal and the sound it makes.

Who Am I?

Say the following animal clues and have your preschooler try to guess what animal you're describing. Can your preschooler make up other clues and have you guess the animals?

For Example:

1. I have soft fur, whiskers and rhyme with hat.
2. I live in the sea and rhyme with park.
3. I eat flies and mosquitoes, and rhyme with log.
4. I slither around and rhyme with rake.
5. I sing and rhyme with word.
6. I eat grass and rhyme with wow.
7. I live in the forest and rhyme with near.
8. I live in the jungle and rhyme with funky.
9. I lay eggs and rhyme with pen.
10. I'm sneaky and rhyme with socks.
11. I say 'oink', and rhyme with wig.
12. I bark and rhyme with bog.
13. I live in the forest and rhyme with hair.
14. I live in the sea and on the land, and rhyme with deal.
15. I swim in cold icy water, and my heavy coat keeps me warm. I rhyme with hair.
16. I'm shaped like a pea, colored bright red, with many black spots to see. I rhyme with rug.
17. I spin a thread to make a trap you call a web. I rhyme with glider.

Answer key: 1. Cat 2. Shark 3. Frog 4. Snake 5. Bird 6. Cow 7. Deer 8. Monkey 9. Hen 10. Fox 11. Pig 12. Dog 13. Bear 14. Seal 15. Polar Bear 16. Ladybug 17. Spider

71

Animal Names & Sounds

Can You...

Play this simple game outside or inside with lots of room! Challenge your preschooler to do the action for 30-seconds or one minute! Or have her choose her favorite and try to guess what animal she's pretending to be?

Wiggle like a worm?

Fly like a bird?

Stamp like a hen?

Neigh like a horse?

Hop like a frog?

Hiss like a snake?

Meow like a cat?

Prowl like a tiger?

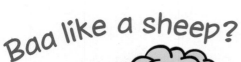

Crawl like crab?

Creep like a caterpillar?

Hoot like an owl?

Moo like a cow?

Oink like a pig?

Growl like a bear?

Roar like a lion?

Scamper like a mouse?

Baa like a sheep?

Buzz like a bee?

Leap like a deer?

DO YOU KNOW WHAT HAS A TRUNK?

Name
_____

Song:
Do You Know What Has A Trunk?
(Track 17)

1

An elephant!

Yes, you were right!
Can you make an
elephant sound?

3

Do you know what has a trunk?

2

Do you know what swings from trees?

4

A monkey!

Yes, you were right!
Can you make a
monkey sound?

A lion!

You were right!
Can you make a
lion sound?

Do you know what's big and brown?

6

Do you know what swims and plays?

8

A seal!

Yes, you were right.
Can you make a
seal sound?

A rattlesnake!

Yes, you were right.
Can you make a
rattlesnake sound?

Do you know what slithers around?

There are animals all around.

Responsibility & Kindness

Easy, Fun Activities to Teach Children Responsibility and Kindness

Songs
- **Dress For The Weather- #11**
- **Just Get Dressed- #12**

My Morning Checklist

Help your child plan his or her morning routine. Discuss and decide upon the tasks that must be done each morning: getting up, getting dressed, brushing teeth, eating breakfast, cleaning the bedroom, etc. Be as detailed or as general as you prefer. On construction paper or copy paper, help your preschooler draw a picture of himself or herself completing each task. Create a simple morning checklist, featuring his or her original artwork, for your child to refer to each morning. To create the checklist, scan the original artwork or reduce/enlarge it on a copier to all fit on one sheet of paper. Display the checklist near your child's room or in the kitchen. Another option is to print or make a new copy each week and encourage your child to check-off each task as it is completed.

Morning Mood

Challenge your child to be dressed by the end of a certain song each morning. Choose one of the songs from the companion CD, set the mood with classical music, or another family favorite "wake-up" tune. Make certain everyone understands the challenge. Consider awarding prizes to each family member if the challenge is met each day for a week!

Morning Reward Chart

Post a **Morning Reward Chart** on the refrigerator or some other prominent place. Use a calendar or create a simple chart on the computer. Give your preschooler a sticker to place on the chart each morning after he or she has gotten ready, without a fuss. Give a prize or treat for every five stickers earned! Or have a small daily reward, and a larger reward on the weekend!

I Choose...Oatmeal!

This challenge might be motivation enough to speed up the morning routine. The first one completely dressed who touches base in the kitchen is the winner—and picks out the morning breakfast for the others in the family.

The Famous Jacket Flip

You'll be a hit with your preschooler after teaching this remarkably easy way to put on your jacket! Lay an unzipped or unbuttoned jacket on its back on the floor in front of you; the front of the jacket should be facing up. Then stand behind the jacket, above the center of the neck opening. With flair and dramatic pause, bend over and fold back both sides of the jacket to reveal and open wide the armholes. Slide one hand into each armhole and flip the jacket smoothly over your head. As you flip the jacket, your arms will naturally slip down into the sleeves and…you're finished! First, have her watch you attempt the Jacket Flip several times. When she thinks she's ready, go for it!

Heat 'Em Up

On chilly mornings, toss the bath towels and even your child's clothes into the dryer for a few minutes to make them toasty warm.

Clothes Kid

Each night, on the floor beside your preschooler's bed, lay out the clothes for the next day in the shape of a person. Include everything, head to toe! The new friend will also double as a sleepover buddy!

Song

• Say "Please" And "Thank You"- #13

Say Please and Thank You

Set an example for your preschooler by saying, "Please," and "Thank You!" You'll teach him to imitate you and respond automatically with the appropriate words. Make a game out of passing objects back and forth and saying, "Please" or "Thank You."

THANK YOU!

Silent Please and Thank You

Please — Make a counterclockwise circle with the right flat hand over the heart.

Thank You (you're welcome) — Touch the lips with the fingertips of one hand, then bring the hand down, palm up.

Family Values

Work together to make a list of principles, rules, and values that your family will try to live by. For example, "We will try to treat each family member with respect." "We will try to always say 'Please' and 'Thank You.'" Or, "We believe it is important to volunteer and serve others." When everyone has agreed to the list, have a signing party where each family member signs his or her name to the document. Frame and display the document where each family member will see it often.

Days Of The Week

Song

Easy, Fun Activities to Teach Children the Days of the Week

- Clap and chant the days in order! Speed up each round until you both fall apart into giggles.

- Chant or sing the days of the week while marching around the kitchen or family room together. Keep going faster and faster!

- Sit together on the floor and pass a ball back and forth. Whoever has the ball must say the next day. Again, see how fast you can complete the challenge!

- If your preschooler is beginning to read, write each day on a large sheet of paper, and stick the sheets around the room. Both of you stand in the center of the room. Shout out a day of the week and have your preschooler race to that sheet.

- Randomly say the days of the week. Your preschooler jumps, moves, or gestures whenever you say a day out of order.

- Display a large calendar on the refrigerator just for your preschooler. Place a sticker on the current day. Help your child keep a simple preschool journal on that calendar —drawing pictures of the weather, activities that day, special events, etc. Talk about the numbers, days of the week, months of the year, seasons, holidays, yesterday, today, tomorrow, before, after, first, next, etc.

1

There are seven days of fun. It's time to learn the days of the week.

3

LET'S SING EACH AND EVERY ONE!

2

SUNDAY

Draw what you do on Sunday.

4

MONDAY

Draw what you do on Monday.

5

✂ -

WEDNESDAY

Draw what you do on Wednesday.

7

TUESDAY

Draw what you do on Tuesday.

6

THURSDAY

Draw what you do on Thursday.

8

FRIDAY

Draw what you do on Friday.

9

- -

SUNDAY

THURSDAY

MONDAY

FRIDAY

TUESDAY

SATURDAY

WEDNESDAY

11

Draw what you do on Saturday.

'10

✂

We just learned the days of the week.

✂

12

Alphabet, Number, Shape Lotto

Cut out the six Lotto game cards on pages 89-92. Cut out the Lotto Caller cards on pages 93-95 and place in a storage bag, envelope, or box. To play, distribute a game card to each player and tokens—small candies, cereal, coins, bingo chips, or tokens from other games. Draw a card out of the bag and say either the color name, shape or letter. Help your preschooler put a token on his card that matches the color or letter that was drawn. Continue until a player has three in a row.

K G ◯

u Q i

y ▲ 6

Z d C

x S 7

⬭ w b

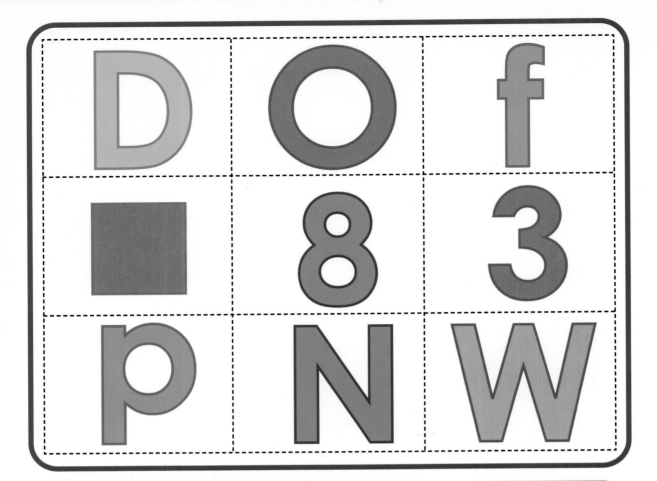

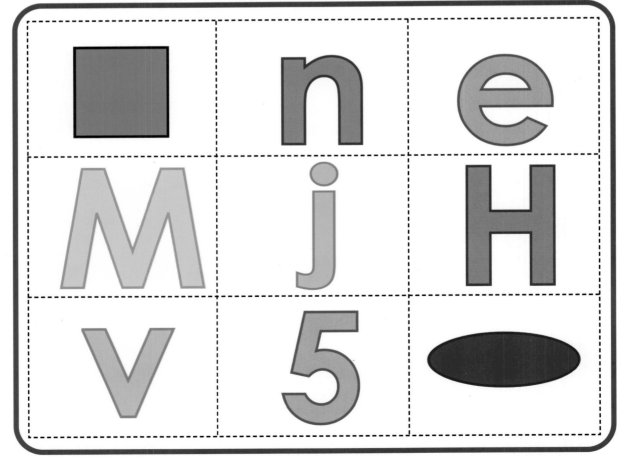

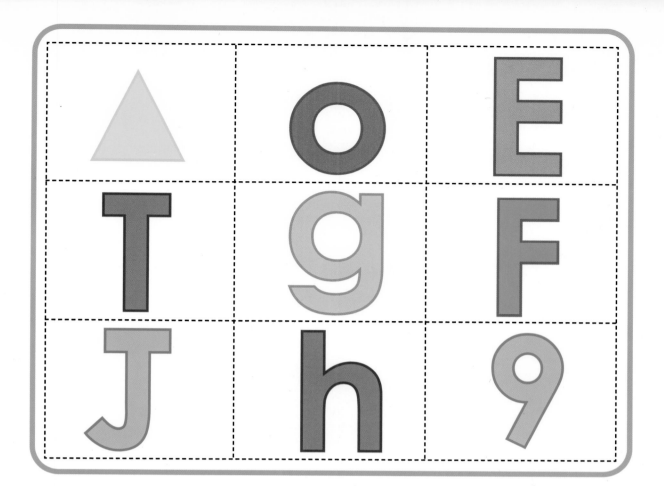

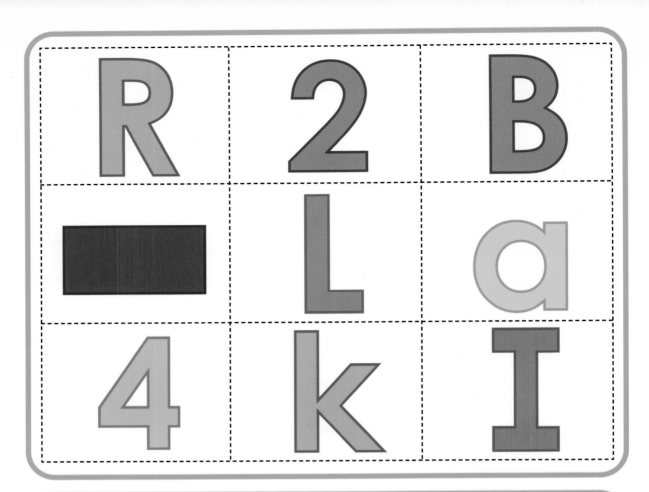

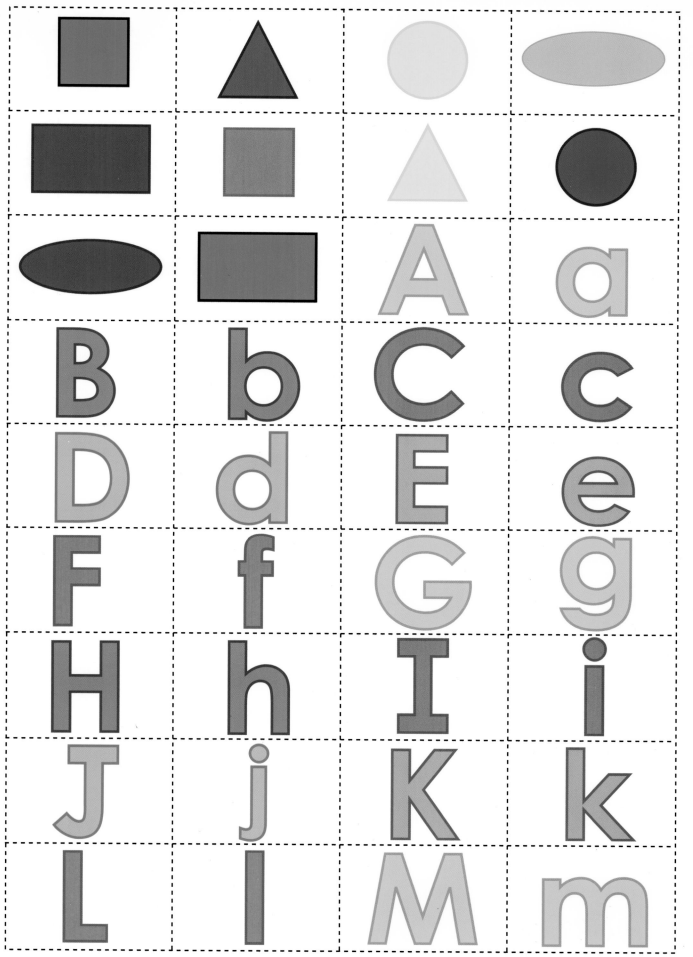

N	n	O	o
P	p	Q	q
R	r	S	s
T	t	U	u
V	v	W	w
X	x	Y	y
Z	z	1	2
3	4	5	6
7	8	9	10